NOW YOU CAN READ....
STORIES JESUS TOLD

STORY RETOLD BY ELAINE IFE

ILLUSTRATED BY RUSSELL LEE

Published by Rourke Publications, Inc. P.O. Box 868,
Windermere, Florida 32786. Copyright © 1983 by Rourke
Publications, Inc. All copyrights reserved. No part of this
book may be reproduced in any form without written per-
mission from the publisher. Printed in the United States of
America.
   The Publishers acknowledge permission from Brimax
Books for the use of the name "Now You Can Read" and
"Large Type For First Readers" which identify Brimax Now
You Can Read series.

Library of Congress Cataloging in Publication Data

Ife, Elaine, 1955-
   Stories Jesus told.

   (Now you can read—Bible stories)
   Summary: Presents the two parables of "The Prodigal
Son" and "The Good Samaritan."
   1. Prodigal son (Parable)—Juvenile literature.
2. Good Samaritan (Parable)—Juvenile literature.
3. Jesus Christ—Parables—Juvenile literature.
[1. Prodigal son (Parable)   2. Good Samaritan (Parable)
3. Parables.   4. Bible stories—N.T.]   I. Lee, Russell,
1944-   ill.   II. Title.   III. Series.
BT378.P8I37   1983   226'.09505   83-13810
ISBN 0-86625-221-5

GROLIER ENTERPRISES CORP.

NOW YOU CAN READ....
STORIES JESUS TOLD

Jesus lived with His family in a village called Nazareth. Mary, His mother, looked after the house. Joseph was a carpenter. He made things out of wood. He worked hard. Jesus helped Joseph each day. People came from far and near to hear Jesus speak about God. He told them stories to show them the way God wanted them to live.

One day, Jesus stood on the hillside. The people sat around Him. He spoke to them about a rich man who had two sons. The two boys worked with their father on a farm.

The elder son
helped his father
plant the seeds.
He helped to look
after the pigs
and the sheep.

The younger son
did not like work.
He lay in the
sun and left the
others to do all
the hard work.

One day, the younger son said to his father, "I do not want to stay here. I want to be with my friends. Give me my share of the farm. I do not want to wait until I am old."

His father was very sad. He did not want to see his son go away. At last he gave him some money. He waved to his son as he went away across the fields. He did not know if he would ever see him again.

At first, the boy was very happy. He bought himself fine clothes. He went out with his friends, eating and drinking.

Soon, he had spent all his money. His friends went away and left him. He was very lonely.

He went to many places looking for work. He was very hungry. A farmer gave him the job of looking after his pigs.

He was so hungry that he even wanted the food that was given to the pigs.

One day, as he sat on the hot dusty ground, watching the pigs, he said, "I will go home to my father. I am very sorry for what I have done. My father looks after his servants better than this. Maybe he will let me be his servant."

Now his father was a very kind man. Every day he went to the top of the hill to see if his son was coming home.
One day, very far away he saw someone coming. He was sure it was his son.

He ran to the servants saying, "Make a feast for everyone. At last my son has come home. Bring out my best cloak for him to wear."

The elder son had been hard at work. He heard his father's words. He was very upset. It did not seem fair. He had stayed at home to help on the farm. He had worked very hard. His brother had wasted his time and his money. Now his father was pleased to see his brother. He was making a feast for his lazy son!

The father saw that his son was angry. He put his arms around him. He said to him, "Come, let us all be happy together. I thought your brother had gone for good. He was lost and now he is found."

Jesus wanted to teach the people that God loves everyone – no matter what she or he may have done.

Another story Jesus told is called "The Good Samaritan."

One day, a trader was on his way from one town to another. It was a long, hard journey. Many people had been attacked by robbers. The robbers hid in the caves dug out of the rocky hillside.

As the man went on his way,
robbers came from behind some rock.
They hit him with their sticks.

The man fell to the ground. He
was hurt and bleeding. They took
all his money and his donkey.
They ran away.

Soon a priest came by, on his way to the Temple. "Is that man dead?" he asked. "If I stop, I shall not be able to go to the Temple."

So he did not stop. He went by on the other side of the road.

After a while, another man came by on his donkey. He was going to sing in the Temple. He saw the poor man lying there in the hot sun. He too passed by. He looked the other way.

A little later, a man from the land called Samaria came by.

He stopped when he saw the man
lying on the ground. He saw that
the man was badly hurt.
The Samaritan washed the man's cuts
and put a clean cloth over them.
He helped the man on to his donkey.

Slowly they went on their way until
they came to an inn.

The Samaritan spoke to the inn-keeper. He said, "Please look after this man. He has been beaten. All his goods have been stolen. Here is some money to pay you. I will come this way again. If you need more money, I will give it to you then."

The Samaritan went on his way.

Jesus said to the people, "Which man would you have to be your friend?" They said, "The Samaritan because he helped the man who was hurt." "Yes," said Jesus. "Now you must go and always help those who cannot help themselves."

Jesus told many more stories. The stories Jesus told are called parables.

All these appear in the pages of the story. Can you find them?

hillside

sons

feast

father

robbers

trader

Samaritan

priest

Now tell the story in your own words.